SKATING OUT OI

Skating Out of the House

ANNA CROWE

PETERLOO POETS

First published in 1997
by Peterloo Poets
2 Kelly Gardens, Calstock, Cornwall PL18 9SA, U.K.

A catalogue record for this book is available
from the British Library

ISBN 1-871471-70-2

Printed in Great Britain by
Latimer Trend & Company Ltd, Plymouth

ACKNOWLEDGEMENTS: some of these poems first appeared in the *Bulletin of the Institute of Mathematical Statistics, Lines Review, London Magazine, New Writing Scotland, Smiths Knoll, Stand, The Honest Ulsterman* and *Writing Women.*

For Julian

Contents

Skating Out of the House

After *Interior with a Lady Playing at the Virginal* by Emanuel de Witte

When I lost the fourth child
the only thing that pleased me, lying there,
was seeing how the chandelier's branches
turned up at the ends,
in just the way that new twigs on the ash
outside the window curl in winter,
bearing buds like black flames.

This was Franciscus' gesture, I remember,
after my Uncle Willem had beaten him
for skating all the way to Harlingen.
Franciscus could not have stopped,
the wind and ice were carrying him, he said.
Of course, they never let me skate like that,
but when he laughed
I felt the wind stinging my cheek.

Our floors are cold, and sometimes I dream
I'm skating on gleaming tiles from room to room.
Successive doorways frame me,
a *mise-en-abyme*, and then
I wake.
        It will be Pentecost before
Bartheld comes home from the Caucasus
with soft, soft rugs for Delft or s'Hertogenbosch.
They say I will not bear him any more children.

These days I often play the *courante*
Father liked so much.
Its final passage fractures
in dazzling splinters.
But when I stand and close the lid
the mirror is frozen over,
the girl I knew
long since gone under the ice.

The Dipper

A pied dipping, midstream:
I let my eye just rest
on a sturdy bird, cream-
bibbed with chestnut breast,
black back, that stutters her own
reflection from a stone.

Of a sudden she slips under
water — a wonder that walks
the burn's bed to meander
from stone to stone — and pokes
for grubs until the mud
comes blossoming in a cloud.

Poised on a rock where the force
tumbles and creams, she is dipping,
dipping; where the water-course
pours its voice without stopping
she goes riding the braided current,
out of the seeing moment

and into her secret places:
the cradling roots of willows
where sunlight laps; dark reaches
under elders; the dazzling shallows;
behind the fall, and best,
the wren-depths of her nest.

Leaving the Walled Garden

Down in the thin backyard she calls the garden
And others call the yard, a child
Helps her grandfather tie up roses.
From time to time their distant voices
Blur, while, in the west, a fleet of clouds
Is building, over the mouth of the river.

There are celebrations down on the river,
Invisible to the child inside the garden.
Frigates mar the water like clouds,
And while the grandfather and the child
Name all the flowers in quiet voices,
The frigates bloom with flags like stolen roses.

The grandfather smiles at the child with cheeks like roses.
Then down the street, like a flowing river,
Come sounds of marching, and singing voices
Whose sadness falls like rain on the garden.
The grandfather comforts the child
Who weeps as she gazes past the walls at the clouds.

He tells her that these are passing clouds.
Their sadness will fade, just like his roses.
You mean it will always come back? asks the child.
Her weeping has carried her over a river,
And now she has lost the way to the garden.
Her ears are full of the singing voices.

Rage, and despair! cry the voices,
While the guns on the frigates puff little clouds
That drift across the sky and over the garden
To fade on the air like grandfather's roses.
And I flow on for ever, moans the river,
Losing itself in the sea. The child

Knows what it is to be a child.
She listens hard these days for the quiet voices
That long ago were swallowed up by the river.
She remembers the flowers — the ones like clouds
Were love-in-a-mist, there were blue cornflowers, and roses,
And big ferns grew at the shady end of the garden.

That child looks pale, say the clouds,
But their voices are borne away like paper roses
As the river goes on holding its own with the garden.

The Marriage-Lintels

Along the garden-backs' high sandstone walls,
A carved slab, now and then — linked hearts, initials,
Year in spiky, eighteenth-century numbers —
Straddles a blind doorway. Each one remembers
Small hopeful fires that blazed like candles
Set in a window where love waits and calls.

Those lovers' eyes have closed, candles blown-out,
But where they lived, life goes on taking root.
Hanging from stopped-up doorways, flowers with bells;
And currant's pungent, vanished tom-cat-smells;
And common fumitory, *smoke-of-the-earth*,
Kindling thin yellow flames as on a hearth.

All but one wall, where the coal-tit's note falls
And still falls as last May she watched warm holes
Fill with mortar while, on the ground, all pulled
Apart, the makings of her small fire cooled.

Mountain Grass Dreaming

A blue unfocused gaze losing itself
In raven-sauntered heights, in scree and icefield,
Sharpens on fingerholds, and hammers glances
Keen as pitons into our crammed shelves.

Books on Scottish mountains he passes over —
Not high enough! and then, specs pushed up
Into his hair's retreating snowline, *Got any*
Books on grass? Climbdown to sheds and mowers,

To Saturday smells of creosote, turps and peat.
I see him obsessively sifting Meadow Grasses,
Timothy Grass and Fescues, gauging ratios,
Balancing texture and nuance, blue with green.

To finger the running seed is to dream the Dolomites,
Climb the Marmarole, whose summits offer
A glittering crown — Croda Malcora, Tofana,
Pelmo, Cristallo — names you can crunch like ice.

Dawn will see him leave San Vito di Cadore
And take the Forcella Piccola. Great Antelao
Soars before him, shoulders ermined in snow,
Pinnacles catching the early sun with glory.

Splintered buttresses stretch in bony spurs
To Borca, and where *brunellen** nod their heads
He sniffs vanilla. By noon he is inching upwards,
The limestone smooth but pitted with useful scars.

His fingers encounter a ledge, the softness of turf:
Another toehold, a shove, and his eyes meet
A level bank of Alpine Meadow Grass,
A greenness not to be found in lowland earth.

Hands closing on empty air, he falls
To thinking it's time his lawn was sown. Come
The summer, it will be time to search, to risk
Everything again; to leave these garden walls.

* A local name for the Vanilla Orchid

Three Desert Poems

1.
Open your hand and let
those things you covet
slip through your fingers like sand.

You may then unencumbered
travel for miles without number —
light as the Jesus Christ lizard

that runs from danger
over the surface of water.
Risking the void

for the chance to embrace
whatever may surface,
you will find yourself fearful, and buoyant.

2.
Open your hand just a little:
there is the darkness from which you came,
the desert roads you travelled

mapped in your palm.
The miles you drank like water,
your footsteps' springy rhythm,

all this your infant daughter
remembers, waking.
Nocturnal and dolorous, hers is a hunger

nothing can fill but hours of walking.
Asleep, she's braced by centuries of rocking;
her breathing, life itself, giving and taking.

3.
Down to our very fingertips
earth has marked us: landscapes,
quick with touch and scored like ploughland, map

a desert-geography, homeland
whose contour-lines the wind
rehearsed in sand.

Making our way from birth to death,
bending upon our path
to touch the earth,

we learn that we are one: her rains
nourish our blood, her desert-plains,
our flesh — this sand; this handful of grains.

The Impossible

Chain-Walk, Kincraig

For Iain

Who knows what we can do? When friends believe
In us, the chrysalis grows tight and splits
And, struggling out, we fly. Your basalt cliffs

Rose up that day like panic. I swallowed hard,
So scared, my two-day migraine slid away.
Yet when I grasped the chains, they were all muscle,

A warmth of linked hands. Then into an hour's
Hauling, up and over-ing, inching downwards,
Toes socketing home, holdfasts to hand.

An afterwards, next year, that you'll remember —
Kestrel leaning upon warm cliff-top air,
Nonchalant grasses, and the glittering Forth.

Sunflowers

For Swithun

Your face shines, grave
and charming as a small moon.
I hear you holding your breath
while finger and thumb encompass
each neat striped seed,
setting it clean in its peat-pot
damp wirh earth, each hole
dibbed by your finger as deep
as one pink nail until,
with crumbs of earth nudged
over each one, we breathe out,
our relief sounding strangely
loud, like a wave breaking.

As pairs of leaves begin thrusting
clear of the earth, we run
with gifts of water; they thrive,
wheeling sunwards on green
wings; the sun draws them
to itself, as the moon the sea,
and the great heads curl and flame.
At night they hang fire, sinking
with the sun, and know nothing
of the moon's rising; as the tide
turns in the bay, rocks
push through the sea. Sun
stirs the slow coronas.

Grown almost twice your height
they are galleons breasting the upper air,
and you, like a small cartographer
busy with charts and rule,
plot their upsurge upon a graph.
In my dream you stand among masts,

your face to the moon in the shrouds,
while towards you black rocks are edging
and crawling, and I, helpless
upon a headland, signalling, signalling . . .
The garden lies gale-wrecked,
and we thresh among broken masts
and wet flower-heads for salvage.

Skin

Was stuff you wore
Carelessly, like clothes.
Not bothering whether it snagged or tore
Or ran, bloodily, to holes. Yours was the
Hands-on approach to life, as though
This sense alone out of the five could tell you
What it was all about. Edges
Were your speciality. The sea-wall,
On a clear day, you could be trusted to
Trot doggedly over. Meetings with steps,
Rocks, kerbs, earth in all its guises,
Unzipped your knees and finger-tips.
Scars along your hair-line notched
A wish to know your subject from the inside.
Weekends, you were a casual visitor
To casualty. Stoical, unsurprised.
Skin, like clothes, would always mend.

It was the other stuff, the nub, the nitty-
Gritty, slipped through your fingers.
Somewhere inside your skin, too
Adolescent-thin for comfort, you
Hid out. You longed to swap it for something cosy,
The furry kind, keeping dormouse-hours
With gerbils. Stroking, stroking their tender plush.
Life on the World Service, *sailing by*.
Your shaved head shouted how tough
You hoped you were. I prayed the really tough
Would somehow miss its pink and shining
Vulnerability. Weekends, helping the vets,
You watched them cut through fur
To the moist throbbings. This summer, when
You let the camping-primus lick your face,
Its breath melted your ears, your T-shirt

Past repairing.
                    Months later, skin
Re-maps itself. Dear awkward one,
I hope this time it fits, though not
So thick, or you so far inside
That you can't hear me say that some things —
You were right — will always mend.

T-Shirts

Perhaps because you're going away
I'm ironing your T-shirts —
The ones I usually hang outside
Face to the wall, away from the neighbours;
Or on the airer, slogans inwards
So that they can't be read. Perhaps I hope
Their shouts will somehow get lost
In the overall neat-and-tidiness.

Of course, it doesn't work. Words explode
Incongruously from laundered cotton
Like well-aimed petrol-bombs.
— If you liked Vietnam you'll love Nicaragua —
— Go ahead, punk! Make my day —
— Instant arsehole. Just add alcohol —
All the silly, sad bravado.

And then an ikon of Marilyn, laughing.
A mouth like a wound. And under it
— Fuck Forever —
I ponder its ambiguity:
Non-stop coitus, don't interrupt us,
A nineteen-year-old's wishful thinking?
My iron swoops on creases, and anger
Sputters up with the steam, spitting
A furious *carpe diem* — Ditch
The future, next year, next week, tomorrow!
Do something now, today, about
This shitty world I didn't ask to be born in.

Gently I smoothe the wrinkles away
From that brilliant, guileless smile.
Slogans can act as camouflage
So no-one sees you wear a T-shirt
Like flimsy armour against despair.

Wasp's Nest

For Ella Macleod and Christopher

As she carried it in to us on a tray
Her clever, weaver's fingers trembled
As if they remembered their work of unravelling;
How, with the dust, there had settled a collective
Silence on the bedroom, enabling her
To slice the nest from the chair's webbing
And to set it gently on newspaper; the few
Faint tremors ceased while she scraped
The chair clean of particles that clung to it,
Crumbs and wafers drifting floorwards.

With its swirls of paper icing
it might be a cake,
a mille-feuilles grey with dust —
but for the brittle litter of wasps,
their fires all out, feelers
like wicks charred black.

The child in the garden cradled his grief.
Fiercely he mourned the wasps that had died.
They swarmed in his head like smoke, making
His eyes smart, his throat begin
To fill with sobs as hard as stones.

When I lift the nest, my hands
weigh its astounding lightness:
a Christmas-bell of chewed
paper as big as a brain;
tiered, turned on itself
like a broad stair, pillared
with spittle;

it inhabits the air
like a citadel, chambered with nectar,
emptied by plague; silence
is settling in combs and cells
like Pompeii filling with ash.

(M)other

I lay too close, my mouth full of your milk,
to wonder if we were the same, of the same ilk.

Two daughters but no son — a definite minus.
Whatever it was he prized, it wasn't in us.

And when his curses left the self-same mark
on both our heads, your arms became my ark.

We moved to France; the red-tiled *salle-à-manger*
heavy with sweet wisteria and anger.

Food was power, served with a slammed mandate:
I gagged on tears, on hated meat, and ate.

Masks — mascara, lipstick's mimicry —
make up for lack: Now I'm like you, I cry.

I must step back to lift your double mask —
snake-locked Medusa/angelic (m)other — to ask

Who are you? What did you find in that mirage
called marriage? When I think of your wasted music, I rage

Yours all went inwards — migraine, back-pain — each mala
teaching me that's what it meant, being a lady.

At night, the piano's grieving tried to mend
our frayed and tattered day, offering an end

of thread from a fugue to follow. Here was your missing
voice; separate and other, it lifted; is singing.

Inside the Earthquake House

there's new and ancient apparatus.
Sand, on the floor, is combed in crisp furrows.

The world's four corners rest
on this as a pair of struts, crossed,
with trios of dollies, north, south, east and west.

Tremors in Samarkand
would send them flying, the spoiled sand
become a map someone could understand.

This quaint simplicity
awes us — in tousled grains to see
the death of thousands, name some cancelled city —

like reading hidden griefs
in mouth or eyes. The pen engraves
each slow, blue hour on paper that moves

too slow for us to sense.
The inverted pendulum tests the silence;
antenna, listening to earth's most secret movements —

it cannot, for all its art,
detect where grief begins, or chart
the desolation of the human heart.

Outside, the notice-board
displays print-outs that record
Armenia's hours, dark where the pen juddered.

Jardin des Plantes

Paris is kind to exiles. Even exotics
Put down roots, flourish. Take this tree,
The only thing in bloom this bitter April —
Perhaps a whiff of scent has already reached you?
Blossom so dazzling everyone runs to greet it
As soon as they come through the gate. Bee-lines vanish
Almost, beneath a tent of flowers so white,
So soft, so sweetly-smelling, at first you miss
A darker note. For even as lovers take
Each other's picture, and laughing children are scolded
Down from branches, I know — I feel it — the tree
Is weeping. Exile and loss. A painful letting-
Go of grief, like snow dropping slow to the ground.
Do you hear a plaintive fairground waltz? The merry-
Go-round is giving rides, and a child astride
Her barley-sugar horse watches the white tree
Go and come back and go and come back and go.

The Sampler

like a garden, is full of flowers;
their cornfield yellows and cornflower blues
are sewn in rows, in rich parterres
between green paths and avenues.

Look how chain-stitch hedges lead
around and inwards like a maze:
arriving at cross-stitch letters, we read
that this was made by Benita Gómez,

10 years of age, who was the pupil
of Doña Gila Escóbar. No child
ever played here or was seen with rumpled
dress to run among roses run wild:

her hours were counted-out French knots,
disposed in silk, confined to linen.
O, I could wish you forget-me-nots,
bare feet, and fields for you to run in

far from this barren embroidery,
Benita! Instead, your perfect flowers
must teach me to drudge for poetry
until my craft's as good as yours.

Visiting the Home of the Brave

1. ARAWAK TUNIC

Columbus took their gentleness
for cowardice, and ear-marked
them and their caciques for slaves.

A note on the wall tells us,
when they were weaving, they always left
a small, deliberate mistake,

as though they understood
how the heart, bent on perfection, ends
trapped in its own web.

Red/black chevrons stutter
their cardiograph
from sleeve to outstretched sleeve,

but somewhere, I tell myself,
will be the invisible blip, one
small, wrong

stitch through which
the weaver's soul
may yet escape.

2. DAKOTA GHOST-SHIRT FROM WOUNDED KNEE

The Cheyenne and Dakota wove
raw muslin into shirts: these were
the shirts for the Ghost-Dance, which,

duly performed, conferred
invisibility on the wearer.
We still believe some form of words

or ritual will come between
us and another's anger. Not seeing
that our invisibility's what's required,

nor that it will be some sudden
memory of past delight that pierces,
leaving this small scorched hole.

Angels Over the Darent

After all, I doubt not but there must be the study of this creation, as well as art and vision; tho' I cannot think it other than . . . the setting of the table before the feast; the prologue of the drama; a dream, and antepast, and proscenium of eternity . . .

Samuel Palmer at Shoreham

He drew from nurturing land as from the breast,
Painting fat hills, and blossom like clotted cream:
The setting of the table before the feast.

His valley's thick with corn. His shepherds rest
As they never did beneath the moon's bright beams.
He drew from nurturing land as from the breast.

Each creature, ear of wheat, and tree's least
Leaf is lit, pieced in the heavenly scheme:
The setting of the table before the feast.

Everything gathered, folded, repossessed.
Eden restored to us might be the theme
He drew from nurturing land, as from the breast.

In Shoreham, as voices wade the Darent, we guess
At angels. Smile as riders splash upstream.
The setting of the table before the feast.

Like Ruth gone out to glean, we find the best
Laid out before us. No prologue and no dream
He drew from nurturing land, as from the breast,
Setting the table, leaving us the feast.

The Bell

after Raphael's *Portrait of Leo X with two Cardinals*

The watchful eyes reveal more than intended.
Intelligence given up to luxury.
Minds sealed off from common human kindness.

All that might unite them — sacred office,
Care of souls, scholarship, or the ties
Of blood (uncle and nephews, two Medicis) —

Is here conveyed in strained, discordant reds,
Giving their flesh the pallor of those who shun
The day. Engrossed, isolate, still, they look

Anywhere but at each other. The gaze
Slides off to impersonal things: the gorgeous book,
The magnifying-glass in the plump fist,

The ornate, tasselled bell. Too late, for them,
To turn to each other, holding out empty hands.
And should they lift the bell, we know who will come.

The Healing of Deacon Justinian by Fra Angelico

for Tony Crowe

A taut white sheet, a water-flask and glass
set on the locker, and under the simple bed
the neat diaconal slippers. Waiting for bliss,

Justinian misses the visitors overhead:
Cosmas and Damian, whom we now recognise
by their red bonnets, have just swum in and tread

a wisp of cloud. We picture his surprise,
waking to meet them, note the jar of physic
each one carries: this time, no-one dies.

This time is also now, where you are sick
in a room as bare as his. Your mind unlocks
a thousand shelves, riffling pages — a quick

flick through India, the army, art-school, *socks.*
How can I meet these people without my slippers?
you beg, wildly, over and over. What shocks

is not the indignities from catheters,
but the simplicity of your incoherence.
To questions plain as this we have no answers.

In Calstock Churchyard

My Bakers baked no bread: inside their oven
Iron reddened to soft, obedient dough,
Was beaten, shaped and tempered to scythe or plough.
As furnace-heat served them by way of leaven,
So heat of imagination serves this daughter,
Glad to follow Benjamin, John and Will,
In hammering verses, forging rhymes, until
The whole rings true, and nothing's out of kilter.

Like gently-rising loaves they're tucked-up here
With Mary, Patience, Grace who, marrying Bakers,
Baked their bread. Close to the forge's violence
They kept a quiet kitchen and, could they spare
The time, might well have written that they were makers
Even in this, bequeathing crumbs of silence.

Kingfisher on the Eden

An afternoon the river phrased for us
In amicable shallows and the cold clear
Of depths we promised we'd come back for later.
After the nettles, the rank *noli-me-tangeres*,
Here was all splash and dazzle and, just for us
Plump naiads slithering on stones, a willow-chair
Where we might let our feet go with the water.
Gnats on the upper reaches; the quickening surface
Nuzzled and slubbed by fish. Always the Eden
Veering between what's seen and hidden; speech
And silence; the real and wished-for. Then, like a flow
Of light, as though conferring all that is given,
Enter the kingfisher, come from the out-of-reach,
The blue unspoken; broaching the here-and-now.

Water-Table

The day you found a circle in long grass
Under the apple-tree and, curious, dug
A little, you thought you had let down sky in a bucket,
As water filled the hole, and your new face
Was a moon, rising. Once, we searched for the place
Where a spring welled on the beach; on baking rocks
I watched you lifting clumps of bladder-wrack
And shells for a lick of water sunk without trace.
Your apple-well, our unquenched afternoon,
Are a palm of water drawn from the Mark's invisible
Welling — sand-grains whirled to a tiny pulse.
I sit and drink, telling the braille off stone,
And feel it everywhere rising — our water-table
Brimming in dried-up springs, in healing-wells.

Note: *The Water of Mark rises at the Queen's Well, Glen Mark, Perthshire.*

Outside the Frame

After *Las Meninas* by Velázquez

If I could paint, I'd have to paint you such
As Velázquez painted Philip and his queen —
A presence everything else implies. Unseen
But for the mirror's distant blur, and reach-
Ing-out of every pair of eyes, to touch
That place outside the frame where we imagine
Flesh-tints and splendid vestments. Roving between
The painting's world and this, their eyes beseech
Us just to stand and be there, making sense
Of fluid light or thick impasto; games
With paint — the artist at work in his own painting,
Brush poised, arrested, everything future tense,
Where canvas, mirror, sun-filled door are frames
That might embrace, like you and me, what's wanting.

Fog

My first sea-fog was Cornish *mizzle* — the word
Ambiguous as the weather. Mornings, I'd test
The air, make sure the breakfast knives weren't crossed,
Hope I had dreamed the storms I'd overheard.
And though some things came closer — gorse, spelling
Its scented heat and sharp defences, scabious'
Blue myopic gaze — they weren't in focus.
At night, I could not see the Eddystone calling.
Since then I've peered through other fogs — *brouillards*
That hid a tongue-tied, stowaway child in France,
And northern *frets* chafing the dangerous Farnes,
And growing ever more dense, this viking *haar* —
You and me in the midst of it like two *a*'s —
And gorse, somewhere, or is it sun, ablaze.

Issio's Well

Under its thick-slabbed slates, heavy as bibles,
Fleshy with navel-wort, Patricio basks
Nose-deep in grasses, headstones, summer's husks.
The chancel cool and dim, where a dragon nibbles
Marvellous fruit: the rood-screen's ripped-out symbols
Made him Satan; but now, like a bat at dusk,
He flits in the fretted lace, through arabesques
Of leaves and roses. Issio's well drops parables,
Chanting the pilgrim virtues: *Be patient, true*
To what you seek, and travel light; drink water
Like a gift; expect the wonderful,
And most of all at home . . . Time to renew
Those vows; on Issio's mossy shelves to scatter
Grasses pressed long since; to say farewell.

Pisa

I know this place, its ring-a-rosy script
Incised in painful clarities of frost:
Landscape of let-downs, of crazy angles; trust
In saturated ground betrayed in inept
Shiftings. Witness the moonlit, skewed cathedral,
The tipsy pudding that doubles as baptistry.
The tower's the worst, its Gothic geometry
Adrift on ground where nothing's on the level.
What's to be done? To prop it in a silo's
To miss the point — Who'd glass-in a rose
Then hold forth on its structure while it dies? —
And building a giant fridge below the Campo?
Gripping it in a block of permafrost?
Better to let it fall. Admit we lost.

Rough Translations

Siberian air, uprisings from the Arctic
Heaving subversive volumes, ran you aground
In Fife. And though you rose as the tide turned,
And vanished, you stuck as two words in cyrillic
Holding a cargo of green and murmurous language.
Your Russian sibilants sang, like forest trees
Before the chain-saw's bitter cadences —
Znamy Oktobry. A flag like a soiled bandage,
Bleeding upon the air as on your streets;
Soaked in meaning, wrung-out like a dream.
On Kinkell Ness, the sea translated from memory,
Breaking in pages, and our hands ached in our pockets
And did not wave at your Russians with unknown names
Who seemed too ordinary for their history.

The Ploughman's Resurrection

The button lay like a seed with the scythed bones,
An embossed 52 in place of a name.
Clearing ground to lay foundation-stones
For some new store, their spades unearthed a fame
You never dreamed of — you with your huge hands
And feet, arthritic joints pressed into fire
From cannon and musket; who died in foreign lands
More miles from Oxfordshire or Buckinghamshire
Than you could tally. Built like the placid horse
That pulled your plough, and in whose wake you'd stumble,
Gulls at your heels, you little thought a hearse
Would bear you and your country's flag to burial;
Nor guessed, since death had set you in their loam,
Your foes would gather you like harvest home.

Note: *In 1986, in Germanstown, Philadelphia, a man's skeleton was unearthed, together with a regimental button. The number on it, 52, showed that the man had served with the Oxfordshire and Buckinghamshire Light Infantry during the American War of Independence.*

Border Country

High over Firle in a furnace wind,
butterflies in their hundreds, skylarks

hovering. Below, high-summer darks
of oaks, and under it all, the chalk.

Before we left, I pressed paper
against our ancient walnut's bark,

scoring it over and over, the pattern
hardening to a lattice of bone.

Back north, the fireweed scatters ash,
the wheatfield's scoured, its whisperings gone.

And on my patch, high time to thresh
our blackening beans, to strip the currant

of pearls. Now summer's over I want
nothing so much as nothing, the mind

cleared, on a war-footing; earth
my border-country, grudging as truth.

Always There

Cerbère, April 1993

They grew beside the track in rows,
Petals like bits of dark-blue rag
On top of spikes like rusty spanners.
Rank and file and ditchback shot past
Into all that had gone before. Later
We saw them beside the road that climbed
Out of town to the brown foothills, the snows.

But this was after the tunnels,
The plaque on the station-wall that held
A handful of names I didn't write down —
Railwaymen, no longer *Morts*
Pour la Patrie, but strictly, impartially
Morts par les faits de guerre.
Europe's at war
At the other end of this blue sea,
And *Srebrenica, Srebrenica*, the train
Had hammered out in France, then Spain.
No space to bury the dead, lying in rows.

Here on the border, the tunnels assume
An older, ominous significance.
Coming down from the station, women with shopping,
Old men in berets, scampering children.
They disappear into the dark
As though this were the most natural thing,
As though the name, *Cerbère*,
Had lost its terrors. We follow a huge
Dog on a lead. It is the only way
To *Centre-Ville* and *Plage*.
But in my head, the poet Antonio Machado,
Still on the run from an older war,
Keeps on crossing the border here, collapsing.

Later that afternoon, we walk through
Another tunnel, emerging behind the town.
The hills step up in terraces. A raw
Brown skin stitched up with vines.
Children are playing with mud beside the road.
They ask us whether we've seen their dog,
Who is white — *Mais non! Il est gris!*
They argue happily while the sea
Looks elsewhere, blue, demure, neutral.
Collioure, where Machado died,
Is just up the coast. Those flowers again.
A kind of lavender. Back home in Fife,
I dig up the name: *Lavandula stoichas*,
Listed by Dioscorides in his *Physica—*
Stoichas: "to stand in rows".

Loaves lie shoulder to shoulder in the baker's.
Oui, madame? The flow of Catalan
Ceases while she serves me, smiling.
We take our *baguettes* down to the front
And eavesdrop on a complicated tale
About this *merlín azul* that turned out to be
Not a bird or a boat, but a fish, *¡fíjate!*
So big they had it stuffed and put in a case.
Cerbère is like a dog with three tails,
All of them wagging. An unimportant
Southern town, not unlike others —
In Bosnia, for instance — that now
Lie shattered, split three ways,
And no-one smiling.

The worst thing that might erupt these days
From Cerbère's tunnels, is water.
The town's main street is concrete passage,
With steps and ramps to raised-up walkways.
Notices warn of flash-floods, picturing cars
Floating out to sea. When rain
Comes roaring off the hills
The street reverts to river-bed,
To what was always there.

Ordnance Survey

The map gives off a whiff of censorship,
The Rother scrawled like a thin blue pencil-line
Through empty spaces. What was here before?
What are these blanks, exploding in our faces?

You have to read between the contour-lines.
A field that's camouflaged as car-park opens
Its mouth like a creek. Only close your eyes
And the tide comes in, filling your head with thunder.
Rain on the tongue, tasting of salt. A reek
Of mud in the drenched air, and sea-birds crying
Thirteen thirsty miles from the sea. Later
You learn that a harbour filled this field; that once
The sea ran into the arms of the hills. But now
You ask, *Did I drown here?* and privately think
The ghost that haunts this place might be yourself.

The mist disorients. Moisture drips from leaves
Like revenant footsteps, leading you on and up
To find the invisible castle. Is it the climbing
Up to water alerts the mind to dis-
Locations, things out of true, banished, gone under?
Resist the shining blandishments of moat
And stone, their wistful, tremulous beauty. The looking-
Glass that underwrites the castle-walls
In tethered, waxen lilies, harmless ducks,
Is armour. Bodyham's lord spiked the great gate
With three sets of portcullis, out of whose murder-
Holes would ooze the lead and pitch, the fluids
Of war. But once you stand inside, the moat's
Invisible, Bodiam seen for what it is.
A spent shell, a withered husk. And in
One tower, a well — water hoarded into
A green malevolent gaze.
                                        Penned in its bed
The Rother mourns, calling the old marsh-levels

In from the ringing farms: Frogshill, Maytham
Wharf, Marsh Quarter; Heronden, Moat, Blackbrook
And Dykes, that used to stand with their feet in water,
Write their high-water-mark between the lines —
And muffled Saxon voices come bubbling up.

Day for Night

For Ferdy and Buffer Woodward

"Whatever else remained the same, the light had changed."
— George Eliot. *Middlemarch*

It was the sudden stumbling into light —
To come from darkened streets into the square,
Finding it arc-lit, humming like a fair,
Strange clothes, and horses, and something not quite right
Under our feet. A roughness we could see
Next morning when we came back to view the set.
A stony, well-compacted, chalky grit
Pressed into sheeting on the ground. Easy
For us to see where pale illusion met
(Outside the ironmonger's) the hard black asphalt
Of the everyday; and strongly we felt
The power of that slight difference underfoot

To make our eyes adjust to their new footing
And see what shimmered there, not as a set,
But Middlemarch — *Widening the skirts of light,*
Via the BBC and rubber sheeting.
You need some props *to see the stars by daylight*
(The kind of thing that Dorothea'd require
Of you, some said); while this odd girl aspired
To find such fires even in the most benight-
Ed spots. Such as the soul of Casaubon
Who, *with his taper stuck before him, forgot
The absence of windows.* Rubbishing others who'd got
It wrong on solar deities, he'd *grown*

Indifferent to the sun. She would retreat
Before the beetling darkness of his mind,
Her own mind's gifts of candle-light declined
(Like this stage lamp-post lying in the street).
And what of Bulstrode, scandal and stumbling-block,

His back religiously turned on truth and light,
Praying to God while pocketing the loot,
Calling it penance. When all his friends forsook
Him one stayed true — his wife, sharing his plight,
Calling him back with "Look up, Nicholas." Pity
And terror we feel for them; terror and pity
For Lydgate. Physician, he could not see they'd blight
His life — her eyes, Rosamund's eyes. So blue,
Presented in a dissecting-dish, they might
Have shown a selfishness like a cataract.
Either, like Psyche, hungry for what is true,
We wake an angry god and feel his spite.
Or we mistake the barber with his brass basin
Worn like a sombrero against the sun
For some false knight who's pinched the shining helmet
Of Mambrino, and chase its innocent gleams
Across the plain, like Quixote. Day for night
We understand, eager for any sleight-
Of-hand that will uncover truth, or dreams.

Stamford, July 1993

There was once a girl

— *Edith's away with the fairies again.*
Thus the Senior Librarian,
Watching you lift a pile of biography
And stumble slowly across to science-fiction.

Am I trying to push you back between covers,
Hoping you may turn out an easy read?
In *Rumpelstiltskin* you might be the miller's daughter,
Locked in an ugly room inside your head.
Despair piles up like flax
But Rumpelstiltskin never knocks.
I think your hair's not right for *Rapunzel*
Although it's the perfect colour —
A fine-spun, princess gold — but there's no length
To shake like a ladder, like dreams, down from your tower.

Trying to read you, I found whole pages
Still uncut, while words went out of focus;
Was it just woolly skirt and stale twin-set?
You moved in a haze, in a blurring of edges.
And adult or children's? Your little-girl hair
And kirby-gripped side-parting
Made you look thirteen, forty, more
Those days when the pills weren't working.

Coffee-breaks, up in the office, you drowned in knitting,
Dropping stitch after stitch as if they burned:
I think of *The Wild Swans* — their sister sitting
Vowed to silence, scorned,
Weaving coats from nettles to break the spell,
Restore the normal; while all our questions fell
Unanswered through widening holes.

It's years since you let fall your wool, Edith,
To write the final page:
Clearer than any word

That downward stroke of your death from off the bridge.
The river poured over you, adding some notes of its own,
And a week's tides tossed you from hand to hand.

Illegible now, you rise
As a faint smell from off the page;
As I open a book where the story begins
There was once a girl . . .

Pittenweem Beach

For Jessica Crowe and Janet Cornfoot

To reach the beach the child likes best
Down to the shore they dragged you
I cradle her, rung over rung, to the shingle
To be swum and stoned at a rope's end
To plowter along the tide-line
For no belief or crime of yours, but rumour
Scouring the ground for bits of china:
Of witchcraft. You were one of the crazed
Throw-outs, shards, crazed like the faces
Refusing to die, at the mercy of men's hands
Of very old women, broken on stones:
That pressed you beneath a door, weighted with stones
Fragments she finds of vanished lives, lifting
"For a quarter of an hour or so"
Sea-weed, unearthing a piece of sky
And then they must fetch a horse and plough
With two birds flying, some writing
And drive it over what they have made
Rubbed, made smooth by the sea
As though to efface it.
And this, we say, we will keep.

Counting

— Do you want to look at two of my legs?

The child is three or four,
his voice half-playful, grave, mysterious.
A swift glance around my desk reveals
bare sandy legs, trousers rolled up
and wet from paddling.
Four miles of beach stretch
from the end of the street —
a shallow, dangerous bay
that each tide works to a new anatomy.

— Do you want to look at two of my legs?

I hear in his troubled counting
anxiety gathering like a seventh wave.
Anchored in front of the Everyman shelves,
his father declines politely, tucks
a battered volume under his arm.
The child goes off to sit in the raised shop-window,
swinging his legs, hugging three books
which his father asks him please to put down.

— I have put them down.
                                On my lap.

He is sailing as close as he dares,
steering by star-words, by clear prepositions;
a child going a voyage around himself,
taking soundings, mapping his coast
with tense, unfathomable arithmetic.

His father comes to the desk
and hands me the book from under his arm,
and I see how the sleeve hangs loose
and empty below the elbow,
with a sail's useless flapping.
I wrap the book and he pays,
makes for the door.
Like a breeze the child forestalls him with

— *Zip my coat up, please.*

They bend to the task, both helping.
I watch them hauling on sheets;
ducking; going about.

Chain-Stitch

For Ella Trotman

She wore this smock to sweep and dust and polish
(Chores I put off endlessly at home) —
A warm red cotton, ample and soft as she was
Under her stays and bosomy handknits; frolicsome,
Given to waltzing around the table, yet gathered,
Yoked to widowhood and childlessness.

A shake of its folds, and there's the moth-dust shining:
Tea with my great-aunt in the tiny flat;
Fresh crab, brown bread and butter, cream on fruit,
And always, the tiny window south to Cornwall —
The way the Sound would glitter, and Edgcumbe woods
Come darkly down to water; bunting and brass
On Navy Days. All this the maidenhair fern
Embraced and veiled, where once she'd watched a ship
Stitching one line of braid away for ever.

I finger the smocking her fingers worked — chain-stitch
In coloured silks, binding us, woman to woman.
I'll wear your smock, but not to dust, and break
The chains that tied you to your chores. Buttoning
Cuffs, I put on your reckless love of life,
Your passionate lust for sweet, exotic fruit —
Who still wept for *dear Phil,* but smacked your lips
At oranges, melons, apricots, peaches, grapes . . .

A Walk With my Father

Follow the woodcutter's track
red-flashed on rock
that zig-zags up the side of Teix*
to the charcoal-burners' floor or *sitje*

Sharp scents of pine and ilex,
the air performing tricks on wires of light —
mirage and incense the guidebook does not mention;
Valdemossa's roofs and towers
beating in waves of silent music;
the limestone landscape numinous on a day
given up to reading maps, while I
go sniffing for signs and portents.

No way for you to guess
that all that shimmering music,
its warm refractive silence,
resembles the conversations we've never had.
Out loud, our voices jangle
like sheep-bells tonguing below in the dry pastures —
a head-down stubbornness, clunking
of endless argument, part of the landscape.

Climbing now. Discussion on seam of rock,
exotic, blue-green like verdigris
crossing the path's red-ochre.
Copper, you say. I think, but do not say,
that it runs like a vein of tenderness
through a workaday marriage, left untapped.
Nor do we speak of the maidenhair fern
glimpsed in the spring's mouth.
That delicate eloquence.

This twig was meant for me — lichen-frilled
it smells of the sea beyond the trees. Up here
all's speckled light and shade, the holm-oaks

57

weaving sun with leaves. A stone-rimmed
mossy platform, smooth as a dancing-floor,
gives us our *sitje*. Stepping inside, I stoop
and loosen the moss with my finger: the smell comes up —
smoke, after fifty years, sharp as a quarrel.

*A mountain in the north-west of Mallorca

At Any O'Clock

For Julian

Deliberate blips, irregularities
    Where all is order, these things tease.
And one thing puzzles me about this church
(St James, with cockle-shells above the door):
    Round every window's rounded arch,
        As though to mark the hour,
    They've laid, between grey blocks of stone,
A narrow band of terracotta — red brick's
        Affirmatory ticks
On silent clocks — setting an extra one,
        Or rather
        Two together
        Here and there,
    Haphazard and irregular;
        Rosily juxtaposed;
          Distinctly odd.
        Are we supposed
To see in this the hand of God,
Poking his finger in between the hours,
        No matter what o'clock,
        Like an oblique
        Memento mori —
The writing on the wall, to say our story
    Is at an end, like King Belshazzar's?

    This is no apocalyptic finger,
    No angry, accusatory digit;
        No harbinger
        To shock us rigid
With *Thou shalt nots* in sixty thousand volts
Hurled down from off the tower in lightning-bolts.
    If these are hands, the way they rove —
    Before, behind, between, above —

Commends itself as love.
Not sacred text
But wholly secular:
A marriage's vernacular,
Perhaps, spelled out in buckshee tiles; relaxed,
Untidy, uninhibited.
Cheering with little reason and less rhyme
The end of British Summer Time?
An extra hour in bed?
Dear terracotta —
Earth and water,
Life's essentials
Shaped by love in warm *You shalls* —
Sex as good as pie-crust
Round the marriage-apple. Sweet, robust,
Spread out in generous baker's dozens,
This is a dish for all our seasons.

Lovers may choose,
These voussoirs seem to say, from this
Deliberate randomness
The hours they use
In time's despite.
For his or her delight
No lover's bound (or he or she is none)
By hours canonical,
By prime or matins, terce or sext or none:
I'll be love's pilgrim, wear you like a cockle
In my hat, my favour
And my favourite, wanton one,
At quarter-to or half-past any hour!
Love's power is exponential;
Extramural, architectural.
Random, essential, odd. The cornerstone.

A Promise of Water

These stones at my door
are dead. Obdurate, bereft
   of water, they yield

hints of life, imprints
of things that breathed, ghosts of roots
   in the mined spaces:

the trace of a stem —
minute segments blocked in jet
   glinting on sandstone;

a pebble of stretched
mudstone pitted as pewter
   where rain hammered it;

and here you can still see
how the twig lay where it fell
   in mire and was pressed

to shadow — a map-
fragment of forked road that leads
   to a lost country.

In sleep, in silence
when night-rain thrums on the ear
   we make the crossing.

The landscape is old,
mapped in bone, in blood's coursing;
   rises like water:

the tree-fern's stone bole,
pineapple-patterned, puts forth
   a fan-vault of leaves,

and sea-lilies rock
gently like paper flowers
from screwstone boulders.

When I wake, the ash
has trawled the sun like a dawn-
fish in its branches;

green, restless leaf-light
lapping my kitchen's white walls;
a promise of water.

The Goodbye-Horse

A noise like distant thunder
heard through the jammed shutters of a room.
Thudding hooves, voices halloo-ing.
Downstairs in the gloom a man mops floors.
I ask, is it cattle being herded,
catching the gleam of a smile:
Here is no cattle. Here is only horses.

Outside, the sun has sucked the colour
out of everything. Light
is a knife slicing the street
into white walls of hurt
whose doorways retreat in darkness.
As in an ancient western
horses and riders
disappear in a cloud of dust.

A single horse is being led down the street.
She has to be destroyed. Her leg is broken.
My son is a vet, takes charge.
I hold her head while he sedates her.
On the ground they spread tarpaulin,
a wink of brass as eyelets catch the sun.
Slowly we coax her on to it.
She stands more quietly now
and I slip my left arm over her neck,
speaking softly while my son
makes ready the lethal dose.

I breathe her warm meadowy smell
and her neck is velvet satin under my fingers.
One eye is very close,
huge in the hot sun.
A mud-brown pool, the white
criss-crossed by thin red veins,

it contemplates me through a straight fringe of lashes.
My arm aches and goes on aching.

I wake with both arms numb,
rigid; hooped on enormous loss;
hands clenched on the mind's bridles.

Forecast

What swims up on screen resembles
The satellite weather-map before
The news. Cloud-cover. Clumps
Of cumulonimbus that scud and pulse.
The sensor glides on gel like an ear
Cocked against my belly.
A hearing mouth, it yammers
Bat-speech into the dark.
Envisioning ear, it catches —
Courtesy of a tanked-up bladder —
Echoes off of cloud-banks.
The night-sky of the womb
Lurches and flickers like an old silent movie.
Voice-over in an Irish accent, listing
Medical terms like *renal artery,*
Corpus luteum, endometrium. Zoom
To another part of the sky, to a moon
Half-buried in cloud. An orbit
Already guessed-at. It shows us
Its dark side, the face that no-one sees.
I look at it hard while Dr F. makes stills,
Clicking around it with the mouse.
And now, time for the news.
As usual, it's bad.

Victory at Guernica

Translated from *Capitale de la Douleur* by Paul Eluard

1.
Fine world of hovels
Of coal-mine and fields

2.
Good faces under fire and in the face of cold
Denial   night   curses   blows

3.
Good faces in the face of everything
Here is emptiness come to freeze you
Your death is to be an example

4.
Death to the spilt heart

5.
They have made you pay for your bread
For sky and earth and water and sleep
And for the poverty
Of your life

6.
They claimed to want mutual understanding
They put the strong on rations   judged lunatics
Gave alms   split pence
They greeted corpses warmly
They overwhelmed one another with civilities

7.
They persist   they pervert   they are not of our world

8.
In women   in children   is the same treasure
Of green spring leaves and pure milk
And endurance
In pure eyes

9.
Women   children   have the same treasure
Deep in their eyes
Men do what they can to defend it

10.
Women   children   have the same red roses
In their eyes
Each reveals the blood we are made of

11.
Fear   and the courage to live and die
Death so difficult   so easy

12.
Men for whom this treasure was sung
Men for whom this treasure was squandered

13.
Real men for whom despair
Feeds the flame devouring hope
Together let us unfurl the last bud of the future

14.
Pariahs   death   the land   and the hideousness
Of our enemies are the self-same
Colour of the night inside us
These we will overcome

In Love With Me

Translated from *Capitale de la Douleur* by Paul Eluard

She is up and on my eyelids
And her hair's mixed up with mine,
She has my own hands' shape
She has the colour of my eyes,
She melts into my shadow
Like a stone into the sky.

Her eyes are always open
And she will not let me sleep.
Her dreams as bright as day
Are strong enough to melt the sun,
And make me laugh, and weep and laugh,
And speak with nothing left to say.

One Moment's Mirror

Translated from *Capitale de la Douleur* by Paul Eluard

It scatters the daylight,
It shows us how thin are the trappings of appearance,
It removes any chance of letting ourselves be distracted.
It is hard like stone,
Like a stone of no particular shape,
The stone of movement and sight,
And its brightness is such that it causes all defences, all masks, to
                                                                buckle.
That which the hand took scorns even to take the hand's shape,
That which once was understood no longer exists,
The bird has melted into the wind,
The sky into its truth,
Ourselves into our own reality.

Remembering Blarney

Strangers' hands marching me
To the parapet — the few swift
Steps back to the guilty child

Frozen over her porridge; a bland
Home Service voice announcing
The death, at nine o'clock,

By hanging . . . Then the cold kiss
Of stone, shocking as a reprieve.
Is that how it was, that day in India —

Finding the snake in your bath
That cured your stammer for weeks?
The shout that brought your sergeant

At the double deafening with the sound
Of childhood's prisons falling.
Your tongue, like mine at Blarney,

A sluice-gate open wide on life, its dapple
And babble. Imagination's scaffolds
Smashed to matchwood, washed away.

Going to Sawrey

The lake like a child's slate; the ferry
Scrawling a chalky wash to the edge,
That minutes will see grow vague, and smudge
In waves, effaced, as weather buries

Detail, rubs out lines; fine
Drizzle turns to Edwardian blur
The distant town, and over-there
Slips into once-upon-a-time.

We watch the lake's perspectives dwindle,
Lapsing to rain-etched miniature.
Grey shore and reeds are water-colour
Warmed by loosestrife's purple candles.

Over the hills, not far away,
Already the landscape starts to prompt:
That bridge, for two small pigs who dreamt
Of a life that held no market-day,

Is gateway to Westmorland, frontier
Of independence, as it was then
For the child entombed in Kensington
With the aspidistras, who kept her clear

Unsentimental eye; tears
Her pigs wept, setting out for market,
She saw let fall as families parted,
And children left for lives downstairs.

She painted life close to the ground.
I see her like a child crouched,
Drawing small clogs outside a porch,
Marsh-marigolds beside a pond.

Each bend the road makes turns a page,
Binds glimpses, sightings, memories
Of waterfalls and farms and trees
Into an eloquent foliage.

Mountains unfold her tales, where death
Waits in ambush for the weak.
But pluck may foil the snapping beak,
And luck or guile the claws and teeth

Of handsome, would-be predators —
For both are heroes, equally
Endowed with courage, wit or folly —
In internecine farmyard wars.

On death, no false propriety.
She shears that tangled Herdwick fleece
To the underlying candour, this
Jane Austen of the nursery.

Consider an admirable parent
Whose words square up to death with vigour:
"He was put in a pie by Mrs McGregor."
But sound advice cannot prevent

The tale of wayward Peter Rabbit.
We always play in the wrong gardens,
Lose more than clothes, lack common-sense.
How shrewdly she draws each foolish habit

In young and old. How well she knew
The human games of cat and mouse.
We shuffle, pilgrims, through her house,
Where mouse-trap, pie-dish, chimney-flue

Send us to water-colours again.
Painting us true, with all our cracks,
She dipped her brush in becks and lakes,
In candid, salutary rain.

Water-Marks

The ledger is crammed with ghosts,
transparencies, thin
as tissue, luminous as skin.
Each pressed flower persists

as nectary emptied of honey,
leaves and stalks
brush-stroked by death; silks
with colours run to rainy

weepings on the page:
tear-stains are umbels,
clusters, stars or bells
grown faint — death as seepage,

oozings, that record
where wild flowers pressed
on paper, flesh on mattress,
in sap or semen, birth-waters, blood.

Allegri in Glen Lednock

Hearing the plainsong rising, falling,
we see the hills for the first time,
how the valley answers itself
like an antiphon.

How the psalmist's grief like the Lednock
cannot be held in, but breaks
in hunger, mercy, love
on stones and turf and burn and ribboning road.

Inside the gliding car
we're lapped in Sistine cloth-of-gold,
but the ear picks at threads,
undoes the buzzard's cry
the stoop to the running fur
death's short discourse.

This music blows from the psalmist's country —
round the next bend, the Lednock shepherd
trudging with reined-in step
behind the flock and tireless dogs,
for whom we go so slow,
obedient to their *miserere*.

The windscreen fills with bobbing backs.
A flow of wool, a burn in spate,
singing the final mile, the home-stretch.
Music fills up every space like water.
The psalmist too comes home, enters his psalm.

Purge me with hyssop, and I shall be clean:
wash me, and I shall be whiter than snow.

As though he had in mind
the mud-caked sheep and car —
all of us inching, folded and pastoral,
until we come where roads and music end.

Dear "Belladonna"

If you were once your true love's Mignonette —
His Mallow, Marjoram, or Meadowsweet,
His Gold of Pleasure and Forgetmenot;
His Flowering, his Round-Fruited, Rannoch Rush;
His Slender Naiad and his Burning Bush;

If, with a change of season, he's grown Nettled,
And Annual Sea-Blite, Love-in-a-mist, creeps cold
Around his heart; and Autumn Squills blow wild,
Filling your glades with gall and Wormwood — Rue
Your loss no more! Don't sit there like a Blue

Or Watery Lobelia, weeping. Swallow
Your London Pride and fetch a Broom or Willow-
Fingered besom. Do some sweeping! Blow
His Yorkshire Fog and Frosted Orache,
Sub rosa stuff, away, with Honesty.

Throw back at him some rougher kinds of flowers —
Bouquets of Goatsbeard, Bladder Nuts, False Cleavers.
Beat him with Fleabane, Club Rush, Prickly Cucumbers.
Try slinging Mudwort. Publish his Petty Whins.
Tell him, a Greater Burdock's yet to be seen!

Declare, by Jupiter's Distaff, his proud mettle
Is all Deadnettle: that you know fine his Foxtail's
Drooping, his Bent is Creeping, his Solomon's Sealed.
Bugle his colours loud in his Little Mouse Ear —
Lousewort! Amphibious Bistort! Stinking Hellebore!

Alice and the Birds

Already she knows the robin, of course;
the blackbirds —Mr Black and Mrs Brown;
the bossy, glossy starlings and jabbing thrush;
but she hasn't quite got the hang of — *bluetit, or great-tit?*
Bending over to get them the right way up.

Grandmother, never one to miss
an educational opportunity, finds her
the *Field Guide to the Birds of Britain and Northern Europe*.
Alice stares through her fringe and sifts
bewilderments of ducks and waders.
She thumbs through buntings, passerines, accentors.
Her gaze hops from page to garden,
and pecks at kitchen-table, bird-table, kitchen-table until
her eyes glaze and she finds her thumb.
Questioned, three-year-old wisdom flies to her aid,
and she opens a page at random —
hoopoe, cuckoo, bee-eater, kingfisher;
declares, she'll *wait till this bird comes.*

And they are coming, Alice:
bee-eaters zithering the air to honey; kingfisher
dropping his gift of a weft of fishbones; hoopoe
to show you how to find buried treasure,
even in a dung-hill; and cuckoo
to teach you (before June) her perfect thirds.
The black-eared wheatear's practising in your ear
his *schwer-schwee-schwee-oo* irregular verbs;
and fan-tailed warbler has sewn you a purse
of carex sedges with cobweb stitches,
to keep your dinner-money in.

In flocks and skeins they're travelling, Alice,
in charm and chattering, murder, muster and siege;
gorgeously-plumed nouns of assemblage
deserting Atlas' snowy fastnesses

and even blanker eleven-plus papers.
Exaltations of larks that rise with the sun;
of plovers, whole congregations; a fall
of woodcock, upon Surrey, of all places.
And just when you thought it was over, and time for bed,
here come flamingos like a flying sunset.
Moonrise; a watch of nightingales.

Workers on the Clyde

After Stanley Spencer

Immense inaudible sound
rains on the shipyards, and surrounds
small groups of men, placid Noahs who bend

to drive pairs of rivets
into another Ark. Light gives them
parts to play in bright Nativities

of steel, or lets them enter
a story where cranes are trees, where girders
overhead make a dense shade, and welders'

tubes like serpents coil
about their feet to make them fall;
a boiler-maker squats inside his whale.

Attendant saints, they turn
from a white-hot body of molten iron
as though from a Calvary that's no concern

of theirs: their piles of marline-
spikes aren't nails, nor that tarpaulin
fallen away from another Easter morning.

Pink as skin, their visors
only serve to show how tender
flesh is; Passions will be enacted later,

elsewhere. Down here, hell's
domesticated, red-hot metal's
dimpled like a chestnut-brazier; cables

twisted by their makers
into the jerseys that they wear.
Set on a ledge, amid the rising clamour

of steel, a teapot stands
and waits for the slackening of hands
that even now are shaping vessels destined

to sail off into slaughter.
Innocents in the theatre
of war, they're painted; one man pouring water

from a hose, intent
yet far away, as though he bent
to water cabbages on green allotments.

A Passion for the Past

The Keeper speaks of their slow disintegration:
"Acid in the wood's to blame," sliding
Out a drawer, "and lack of ventilation."

He lifts a sheet of glass. "These are the worst.
Actually, these aren't Scottish at all, but Irish,
Mostly beyond repair, just piles of dust."

He leaves me while he goes to collect a child.
Set out upon the table, parish by parish,
Neatly labelled, they are for all the world

Like crumbling biscuits someone forgot to eat.
Faculty chemists have saved a few, restoring
Pewter's dull respectable shine — meet,

Right, and stamped with bounden duty: *This token
Permits the bearer to come to the Lord's table.*
Rural communions, handed down in broken

Crumbs. Passwords crossing the streets of ravaged
Towns. Squinting at ancient parish labels,
I find *Dungannon.* Then *Inniskillen.* Badged

With blight, they are exploding slowly down
The decades, pat-a-cake *D*'s and *I*'s swelling
Into invisibility. Soon, no-one

Will make out *Do this in remembrance
Of me,* or *Let a man examine himself.*
They will have turned to leaden frost, elements

Transubstantiating into a dust
So heavy that my breath can't make it move.
And yet, though perished, substance won't be lost.

"A specially created database
Will store these parish relics, recording local
Features, like an embossed church or chalice,

For posterity. "The Keeper of
The University Collections bustles
In with tiny daughter — human love's

Mysterious all-transforming power expressed
Already in her arms, clutched tight about
A headless doll. That contact with the past,

Her father says, — "to touch it" — is what he finds
Enthralling. He shows me out, then innocently
Calls, "Oh, don't forget to wash your hands."

Heartstring Theory

"Important class of random processes"
Arguably might include the concept, *love*:
If we consider all its fine excesses,
No wonder mathematicians long to prove

Its force is calculable, and thus REDUCE
The damage of its *vector field*. We fall
In love, we say, as though we had no choice,
Or choice itself were purely accidental.

Life hurls us up to fall like 'Pick-a-Sticks'
(That's *fibre-bundles* to a statistician).
"Statistics?" I hear you cry, "Ah yes, *Stochastics!*"
For how we land depends on *Brownian motion.*

Like water-droplets in a *jet (jet d'eau*
From Monsieur Ehresmann), we rise as one,
In speed, élan. Falling, we write the credo
Of statistical asymptotics: *phylon*

Will seek its *phyla*, drawn by *Taylor strings*
(Heartstrings), and *scalar strings*. With each trajectory
Mapped before it happens, and hapless drifting
Towards one face *preferred point geometry,*

Symbolic Itô calculus is invoked
To plumb the question in a pair of eyes;
Into T^{th}*-order connection* smiles are *yoked,*
Computed in *tensorial indices.*

Well then, let's find *cotangent fields* to lie in;
Explore *stochastic differentials*; practise
Those *yokes* and try some *intertwinin'* —
Drift towards that good old *bracket process.*

Let *quasi-jets* draw *string-fields* overhead.
I hear the sea below us casting runes.
And gently, among the great mathematical dead,
Napier the Scot laughing, rattling his Bones.

Tracing the Child

Dazzling chirp
The cricket's song bursts onto screen.
All local colour, incident —
Grand Teton's blue Wyoming peaks,
The sagebrush whisperings after dark —
Have been deleted.
Summer's voice
Is yellow light,
A silent trace
Sputtering along time's axis like a fuse.
Those frenzied stridulations have become
Small sunbursts we can measure.
Yet who would guess
A single syllable could hold
These seventy thousand pulsings of desire?

Only the child, perhaps, who holds the moment
Like a glass of water to the light,
Letting its facets compose
Grandparents' voices;
A saw coughing through wood;
Shelled peas riddling into a basin,
Joy like a rising note.
Cheek creased by grass
She breathes in cricket-song;
Becomes honeysuckle aching under
A weight of bees; shapes her throat
To a seagull's cry.
The sun pokes open her eyelids
And through the grass-stalks shows her
A butterfly-wing of ocean,
Sky-coloured, common-blue;
More points of sparkling light than she can count.

A brightness I find again some mornings
Skirting the kitchen-step — slug-tracks;
Slime like a trail wrung from the self;
A paradigm of memory leading back
To the slow, evasive child I had forgotten.
Sticky with secrets, without a shell,
She leaves this silent trace
Of vanished Atlantic sparkle.